Saint Patrick's Day Food Ideas Perfect for A Party

Sweet Ways to Celebrate St. Patrick Day

Copyright © 2021

DEDICATION

Contents

Main Dishes

1. Irish Potato Bites

Ingredients

20 Red potatoes, small (golf ball size)

1/2 cup Corned beef

1/4 cup Cheddar cheese, shredded

1 tablespoon Butter, melted

1/8 teaspoon Salt

Sour cream, (optional)

Instructions

1. Fill a large pot with water and bring it to a boil.

2. Add potatoes and boil until they are fork tender.

3. Preheat oven to 400°F

4. Once potatoes are cooked and have cooled cut each one in half and cut a small slice off of the rounded end so the potato can sit up.

5. Scoop out the inside of each potato half saving the potato insides in a bowl.

6. Add cheese, corned beef, butter to the bowl with the saved potato insides.

7. Salt mixture to taste. Also sprinkle some salt over the potato halves.

8. Scoop mixture into potato halves and then place them on a baking

sheet.

9. Place baking sheet in oven for 10 minutes.

10. Remove from oven and serve with a dollop of sour cream.

Nutrition Facts

Per serving: 5bites, calories: 106kcal, carbohydrates: 13g, protein: 4g, fat: 5g, saturated fat: 2g, cholesterol: 17mg, sodium: 233mg, potassium: 300mg, fiber: 1g, vitamin a: 100iu, vitamin c: 18.2mg, calcium: 40mg, iron: 0.7mg

2. Stout & Honey Beef Roast

Ingredients

12 small red potatoes (about 1-1/2 pounds), scrubbed

6 to 7 medium carrots (about 1 pound), peeled and cut into 1/2-inch pieces

2 medium onions, quartered

1 boneless beef chuck roast (4 pounds), trimmed

1 can (14-1/2 ounces) beef broth

1 cup beer or additional beef broth

1/2 cup honey

3 garlic cloves, minced

1 teaspoon dried marjoram

1 teaspoon dried thyme

1/2 teaspoon salt

1/2 teaspoon pepper

1/4 teaspoon ground cinnamon

2 tablespoons cornstarch

1/4 cup cold water

Minced fresh thyme, optional

Instructions

1. Place potatoes, carrots and onion in a 5-qt. slow cooker. Cut roast in half; transfer to slow cooker. In a small bowl, combine next 9 ingredients; pour over top. Cook, covered, on low until meat and vegetables are tender, 8-10 hours.

2. Slice beef and keep warm. Strain cooking juices, reserving vegetables and 1 cup liquid. Skim fat from reserved liquid; transfer liquid to a small saucepan. Bring to a boil. Combine cornstarch and water until smooth; gradually stir into juices. Bring to a boil; cook and stir until thickened, about 2 minutes. Serve with beef and vegetables. If desired, top with fresh thyme.

Nutrition Facts

1 serving: 361 calories, 15g fat (6g saturated fat), 98mg cholesterol, 340mg sodium, 25g carbohydrate (14g sugars, 2g fiber), 31g protein.

3. Irish Beef Stew

Ingredients

3 tbsp. extra-virgin olive oil, divided

2 lb. beef chuck stew meat, cubed into 1" pieces

Kosher salt

Freshly ground black pepper

1 onion, chopped

2 medium carrots, peeled and cut into rounds

2 stalks celery, chopped

3 cloves garlic, minced

3 medium russet potatoes, peeled and cut into large chunks

4 c. low-sodium beef broth

1 (16-oz.) bottle Guinness

2 tsp. fresh thyme

Freshly chopped parsley, for serving

Instructions

1. In a large Dutch oven over medium heat, heat 2 tablespoons oil. Season beef with salt and pepper, then add to pot and cook on all sides until seared, 10 minutes, working in batches if necessary. Transfer beef to a plate.

2. In same pot, add remaining tablespoon oil and cook onion, carrots, and celery until soft, 5 minutes. Season with salt and pepper. Add garlic and cook until fragrant, 1 minute.

3. Add beef back to Dutch oven, then add potatoes, broth, beer, and thyme. Bring to a boil, then reduce heat to a simmer. Season with salt and pepper. Cover and let simmer until beef and potatoes are tender, 30 minutes.

4. Garnish with parsley before serving.

4. Slow Cooker Corned Beef And Cabbage Stew

Ingredients

2 pounds corned beef cut into bite sized pieces

4 large potatoes cut into large pieces

2 stalks celery chopped

1 white onion chopped

Saint Patrick's Day Food Ideas Perfect for A Party

1 bag baby carrots 16 oz

1/2 head cabbage cut into small wedges

3 cups beef broth

1 Tablespoon Worcestershire sauce

2 Tablespoons McCormick® Pickling Spice

1 Teaspoon McCormick® Garlic Powder

1/2 Teaspoon McCormick® Paprika

1 teaspoon salt

1 teaspoon pepper

1 Tablespoon cornstarch optional

Chopped Parsley and additional salt and pepper for garnish

Instructions

1. Add corned beef, potatoes, celery, onion, and cabbage to your slow cooker.

2.   In a medium sized mixing bowl combine beef broth, worchestershire sauce, pickling spice, garlic powder, paprika and salt and pepper. Pour over the meat and veggies.

3. Cook on low for 8-10 hours or high for 5-6 until the vegetables are tender and meat is cooked throughout.

4. Add salt and pepper to taste and garnish with chopped parsley.

5. Corned Beef and Cabbage

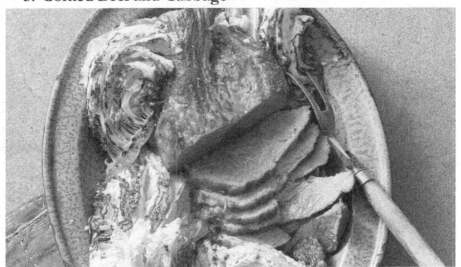

Ingredients

1 3-lb piece corned beef (with spice packet, if included)

1 12-oz bottle pale ale

1 medium onion

2 cloves garlic

2 dried bay leaves

2 tbsp. olive oil

1 small head green cabbage (about 1 3/4 lb), cut into 8 wedges

Chopped parsley, for serving

Instructions

1. Place corned beef in large pot. Add beer, onion, garlic, bay leaves, 1½ cups water, and contents of spice packet (if included) and bring to a boil. Reduce heat and simmer, covered, until tender and easily pierced with a fork, 2½ to 3 hours.

2. Thirty minutes before corned beef is finished, heat oven to 425°F. Heat a large cast iron skillet on medium-high heat. Season cabbage with ½ teaspoon each salt and pepper. In batches, add 1 tablespoon oil and 4 pieces cabbage and cook until golden brown, 3 minutes per side; transfer to baking sheet and repeat.

3. Transfer beef to foil-lined baking sheet. Transfer beef and cabbage to oven and roast until cabbage is just tender and beef has browned, 12 to 15 minutes.

4. Transfer beef to cutting board and thinly slice. Serve with roasted cabbage and sprinkle with parsley, if using.

6. Guinness and beef empanadas

Ingredients

1 lb ground beef

0.5 cup onion, finely chopped

2 medium-sized potatoes, diced

1/2 teaspoon dried thyme

0.5 cup peas

Saint Patrick's Day Food Ideas Perfect for A Party

1 bottle Guinness Stout

2 tablespoons of Worcestershire sauce

Salt and pepper, to taste

2 packs of deep-dish pastry shells (4 shells total) or your favorite pie pastry recipe doubled.

Milk

Instructions

1. Pre-heat oven to 375 degrees Fahrenheit.

2. Grease a baking pan with cooking spray and set aside.

3. In a skillet over medium-high heat, brown the beef and onion then stir in the vegetables, thyme, Guinness, Worcestershire sauce and seasonings.

4. Bring the mixture to the boil.

5. Reduce heat and simmer for 7 to 8 minutes or until the vegetables are tender.

6. Roll out the pastry dough and cut out 16 – 5-inch rounds and 16 – 5.5-inch rounds.

7. Spoon the filling onto five-inch rounds, brushing milk around the edges and cover with the 5.5-inch rounds and press with a fork to seal.

8. Bake for 12 to 15 minutes and serve warm.

9. Enjoy!

7. Irish Stew

Ingredients

2 medium-sized onions, chopped

Oil, for frying

1-ounce butter

1 sprig dried thyme

2 1/2 pounds best end of lamb neck, cut into large pieces

7 carrots, chopped lengthways into 2-inch pieces

2 tablespoons pearl barley

5 cups Chicken Stock, recipe follows

Salt (recommended: Fleur du Sel)

Freshly ground black pepper

1 bouquet garni (parsley, thyme, and bay leaf)

12 medium potatoes

1 bunch parsley, leaves finely chopped

1 bunch chives

Stock:

Chicken carcass

1 onion

4 cups water

3 stalks celery, roughly chopped

Bay leaf

Salt and freshly ground black pepper

Herb Butter:

1 stick butter

1 small bunch parsley, finely chopped

1 small bunch chives, finely chopped

1 sprig thyme

Instructions

1. In a large heavy-bottomed saucepan, cook the onions in oil and butter, on medium-high heat until they are translucent. Add the dried thyme and stir. Add the lamb and brown on a high heat to seal in juices. Add carrots, and pearl barley. Pour in the Chicken Stock so that it almost covers the meat and vegetables. Season with salt and pepper,

and add Bouquet garni. Cover and cook on low heat for 2 hours, being careful not to boil. Place potatoes on top of the stew, cover and cook for 30 minutes until the meat is falling beautifully off the bones and the potatoes are fork tender.

2. Serve the stew in large flat soup bowls, and drizzle Herb Butter over the potatoes or garnish with parsley and chives.

3. Stock:

Preheat the stockpot. Combine ingredients in a large heavy-bottomed saucepan and cover with water. Bring to boil and simmer for approximately 30 minutes. Then let it cool down and skim off the fat.

4. Herb Butter:

Melt butter in a small saucepan. Add parsley, chives and thyme.

8. St. Patrick's Day Fried Cabbage

Ingredients

2 tablespoons unsalted butter

4 slices bacon (about 3 ounces) sliced crosswise into 1/2-inch strips

1 medium onion, diced

3 cloves garlic, sliced

1/2 large head green cabbage, quartered, cored and sliced crosswise into 1/2-inch-thick slices

Kosher salt and freshly ground black pepper

2 teaspoons Worcestershire sauce

Instructions

1. Place the butter and the bacon in a large Dutch oven or pot with a lid over medium-high heat. Cook, stirring occasionally, until bacon is lightly browned and crisp, 7 to 8 minutes (lower the heat if the bacon begins to get too dark). Using a slotted spoon, remove the bacon to a paper-towel-lined plate and reserve (do not wipe out pot).

2. Add the onion, garlic, and 1/2 teaspoon salt to the pot, stirring frequently with a wooden spoon and scraping up any browned bits from the bottom of the pan. Cook until the onion is very soft, about 8 minutes.

3. With the heat at medium-high, add the cabbage, 1 teaspoon salt, and 1/4 teaspoon black pepper. Stir until the cabbage starts to soften, 5 minutes. Reduce heat to medium-low or low and cook, covered, until

the cabbage is very tender, with a little bit of texture remaining in the thicker rib pieces, 12 to 15 minutes, stirring occasionally to make sure the bottom isn̨t getting too dark.

4. Uncover the pot and increase heat to high. Add the Worcestershire sauce and stir for about a minute. There should be almost no liquid in the pot. Add more salt and pepper, if necessary, transfer to a serving bowl and top with the reserved bacon bits.

9. Potato Leek Soup

Ingredients

1 tbsp. olive oil, plus more for serving

4 leeks (white and light green parts only), sliced into half-moons

2 cloves garlic, finely chopped

Saint Patrick's Day Food Ideas Perfect for A Party

1 bulb fennel, cut into 1/4-in. pieces

1 stalk celery, thinly sliced

Kosher salt and pepper

3 c. leftover mashed potatoes

6 c. low-sodium chicken broth

4 sprigs fresh thyme

1 bay leaf (optional)

1 tbsp. lemon juice (optional)

Instructions

1. Heat oil in large pot on medium. Add leeks, garlic, fennel, and celery, season with 1/4 teaspoon salt and cook, covered, stirring occasionally, until very tender, 13 to 15 minutes.

2. Add mashed potatoes, broth, thyme, and bay leaf and simmer, stirring occasionally, until heated through, about 5 minutes.

3. Remove and discard thyme and bay leaf. Using immersion blender (or standard blender, in batches), puree soup until smooth. Stir in lemon juice and serve with cracked pepper and drizzle of oil if desired.

Nutritional Information:

About 370 calories, 16 g fat (6 g saturated), 12 g protein, 785 mg sodium, 49 g carb, 6 g fiber

Salad Recipes

1. Rainbow Fruit Salad

Ingredients

2 large firm bananas, sliced

2 tablespoons lemon juice

2 cups seeded cubed watermelon

2 cups fresh or canned pineapple chunks

1 pint fresh blueberries

3 kiwifruit, peeled and sliced

1 pint fresh strawberries, halved

6 ounces cream cheese, softened

1/3 cup confectioners' sugar

2 tablespoons fresh lime juice

1/2 teaspoon grated lime zest

1 cup heavy whipping cream, whipped

Instructions

1. Toss bananas in lemon juice; place in a 4-qt. glass serving bowl. Add remaining fruit in layers.

2. In a bowl, beat cream cheese until smooth. Gradually add sugar and the lime juice and zest. Stir in a small amount of whipped cream; mix well. Fold in remaining whipped cream. Spread over fruit. Chill until

serving.

Nutrition Facts

3/4 cup: 123 calories, 7g fat (5g saturated fat), 22mg cholesterol, 31mg sodium, 14g carbohydrate (10g sugars, 2g fiber), 1g protein.

2. Pistachio Mallow Salad

Ingredients

1 carton (16 ounces) whipped topping

1 package (3.4 ounces) instant pistachio pudding mix

6 to 7 drops green food coloring, optional

3 cups miniature marshmallows

1 can (20 ounces) pineapple tidbits, undrained

1/2 cup chopped pistachios or walnuts

Additional whipped topping, optional

Instructions

1. In a large bowl, combine whipped topping, pudding mix and food coloring if desired.

2. Fold in the marshmallows and pineapple.

3. Cover and refrigerate for at least 2 hours.

4. Just before serving, top with additional whipped topping if desired, sprinkle with nuts.

Nutrition Facts

3/4 cup: 236 calories, 9g fat (7g saturated fat), 0 cholesterol, 140mg sodium, 35g carbohydrate (23g sugars, 1g fiber), 2g protein.

Cake Recipes

1. Shamrock Cutout Pound Cake

Ingredients

2 packages (16 ounces each) pound cake mix

10 drops green food coloring

1/2 teaspoon peppermint extract

Glaze:

1 cup confectioners' sugar

1/8 teaspoon peppermint extract

3 to 5 teaspoons 2% milk

Instructions

1. Preheat oven according to package directions. Grease a 9x5-in. loaf pan. Prepare one package cake mix according to package directions, adding food coloring and extract before mixing batter. Transfer to prepared pan. Bake and cool as package directs.

2. Cut cooled cake into 1-in.-thick slices. Cut slices with a 2-1/2-in. shamrock-shaped cookie cutter (save remaining cake for another use). Stand shamrock slices at an angle in a greased 9x5-in. loaf pan.

3. Prepare remaining cake mix according to package directions. Pour

batter around and over shamrock slices. Bake and cool as package directs.

4. For glaze, in a small bowl, mix confectioners' sugar, extract and enough milk to reach desired consistency. Pour glaze over cake, allowing some to flow over sides.

Note:

Remaining pound cake may be cubed and served in dessert dishes, layered with warm fudge sauce. Top with chopped mint Andes candies.

Nutrition Facts

1 slice: 228 calories, 7g fat (4g saturated fat), 43mg cholesterol, 181mg sodium, 40g carbohydrate (26g sugars, 1g fiber), 3g protein.

2. Savory Party Bread

Ingredients

1 unsliced round loaf sourdough bread (1 pound)

1 pound Monterey Jack cheese

1/2 cup butter, melted

1/2 cup chopped green onions

2 to 3 teaspoons poppy seeds

Instructions

1. Preheat oven to 350°. Cut bread widthwise into 1-in. slices to within 1/2 in. of bottom of loaf. Repeat cuts in opposite direction. Cut cheese into 1/4-in. slices; cut slices into small pieces. Place cheese in cuts in bread.

2. In a small bowl, mix butter, green onions and poppy seeds; drizzle over bread. Wrap in foil; place on a baking sheet. Bake 15 minutes. Unwrap; bake until cheese is melted, about 10 minutes longer.

Test Kitchen Tips

1. Take a page from the "magnificent everything bagel" by adding 1 teaspoon each of dried garlic, onion and sesame seeds to the butter mixture.

2. Get little hands involved by having them place cheese in the bread. Here are more kitchen tasks for kids of any age.

3. Make it your own by switching up the cheese, customizing seasonings, and adding meaty mix-ins. Bacon, diced salami or ham with

sliced olives are all great choices.

4. Keep these essential bread baking supplies handy for this recipe.

Nutrition Facts

1 serving: 481 calories, 31g fat (17g saturated fat), 91mg cholesterol, 782mg sodium, 32g carbohydrate (1g sugars, 2g fiber), 17g protein.

3. Irish Apple Cake with Custard Sauce

Ingredients

For The Cake:

3 C. Flour

2 t. Baking Powder

⅛ t. Salt

¼ t. Cloves, ground

¼ t. Nutmeg, ground

6 oz. Butter, (cold is fine)

¾ C. Sugar

4 large Granny Smith apples(I used golden delicious to great effect)

2 Eggs

¾ C. Milk

2 T. Sugar(for sprinkling on top of cake)

For The Custard:

6 large Egg Yolks

6 T. Sugar

1½ C. Whole Milk

1½ t. Vanilla

Instructions

For The Cake:

1. Grease and flour an 8" or 9" round springform pan. Using an 8" pan will give you a taller cake.

2. Preheat the oven to 375 degrees.

3. Sift the flour, baking powder, salt, cloves and nutmeg into a large mixing bowl. Make sure the bowl is very large to allow room for the apples to be folded in.

4. Cut the butter into the flour using your fingers or a pastry cutter until the mixture resembles fine crumbs.

5. Add the ¾ C. sugar to the flour mixture and mix in.

6. Peel the apples and slice them into uniform pieces. This cake works best and gets that 'chunky apple look' if the slices are about ¼" wide and then cut into 3 pieces.

7. Toss the apples into the flour mixture and combine them thoroughly.

8. In a separate bowl, beat the eggs and milk together. Add to the apples and flour and mix in with a large spatula until just combined. Batter will be thick and dough-like.

9. Transfer the dough into the prepared cake pan and flatten the top surface using the back of your spatula.

10. Sprinkle the sugar over the top of the cake.

11. Bake for 45-50 minutes. Test the center for doneness. The top of the cake should be golden brown. Serve slices with custard sauce.

For The Custard Sauce:

Note: this sauce is not a thick, pudding like sauce. It should have a pour-able, just thickened consistency when done.

1. Place the egg yolks and sugar in a bowl and whisk until pale yellow, 2-3 minutes. Place the milk in a medium saucepan and bring just to a boil. Slowly whisk the hot milk into the egg/sugar mixture. Transfer the mixture back to the saucepan and stir over medium heat until custard thickens, about 4 minutes. Custard should be thick enough to coat the back of a spoon. Mix in the vanilla. Transfer to bowl or serving saucer.

2. Serve warm or cold over apple cake.

4. Reuben Rounds

Ingredients

1 sheet frozen puff pastry, thawed

6 slices Swiss cheese

5 slices deli corned beef

1/2 cup sauerkraut, rinsed and well drained

1 teaspoon caraway seeds

1/4 cup Thousand Island salad dressing

Instructions

1. Preheat oven to 400°. Unfold puff pastry; layer with cheese, corned beef and sauerkraut to within 1/2-in. of edges. Roll up jelly-roll style. Trim ends and cut crosswise into 16 slices. Place on greased baking sheets, cut side down. Sprinkle with caraway seeds.

2. Bake until golden brown, 18-20 minutes. Serve with salad dressing.

Nutrition Facts

1 appetizer: 114 calories, 7g fat (2g saturated fat), 8mg cholesterol, 198mg sodium, 10g carbohydrate (1g sugars, 1g fiber), 3g protein.

5. Chocolate Guinness Cake

Ingredients

1 cup Guinness (dark beer)

1/2 cup butter, cubed

2 cups sugar

3/4 cup baking cocoa

2 large eggs, beaten, room temperature

2/3 cup sour cream

3 teaspoons vanilla extract

2 cups all-purpose flour

1-1/2 teaspoons baking soda

Topping:

1 package (8 ounces) cream cheese, softened

1-1/2 cups confectioners' sugar

1/2 cup heavy whipping cream

Instructions

1. Preheat oven to 350°. Grease a 9-in. springform pan and line the bottom with parchment; set aside.

2. In a small saucepan, heat beer and butter until butter is melted. Remove from the heat; whisk in sugar and cocoa until blended. Combine the eggs, sour cream and vanilla; whisk into beer mixture.

Combine flour and baking soda; whisk into beer mixture until smooth. Pour batter into prepared pan.

3. Bake until a toothpick inserted in the center comes out clean, 45-50 minutes. Cool completely in pan on a wire rack. Remove cake from the pan and place on a platter or cake stand.

4. In a large bowl, beat cream cheese until fluffy. Add confectioners' sugar and cream; beat until smooth (do not overbeat). Frost top of cake. Refrigerate leftovers.

Nutrition Facts

1 slice: 494 calories, 22g fat (13g saturated fat), 99mg cholesterol, 288mg sodium, 69g carbohydrate (49g sugars, 2g fiber), 6g protein.

6. Savory Potato Skins

Ingredients

4 large baking potatoes (about 12 ounces each)

3 tablespoons butter, melted

1 teaspoon salt

1 teaspoon garlic powder

1 teaspoon paprika

Optional: Sour cream and chives

Instructions

1. Preheat oven to 375°. Scrub potatoes; pierce several times with a fork. Place on a greased baking sheet; bake until tender, 1-1-1/4 hours. Cool slightly.

2. Cut each potato lengthwise in half. Scoop out pulp, leaving 1/4-in.-thick shells (save pulp for another use).

3. Cut each half shell lengthwise into quarters; return to baking sheet. Brush insides with butter. Mix seasonings; sprinkle over butter.

4. Broil 4-5 in. from heat until golden brown, 5-8 minutes. If desired, mix sour cream and chives and serve with potato skins.

Nutrition Facts

1 piece: 56 calories, 2g fat (1g saturated fat), 6mg cholesterol, 168mg sodium, 8g carbohydrate (0 sugars, 1g fiber), 1g protein.

7. Cheddar Ham Cups

Ingredients

2 cups (8 ounces) finely shredded cheddar cheese

2 packages (2-1/2 ounces each) thinly sliced deli ham, chopped

3/4 cup mayonnaise

1/3 cup real bacon bits

2 to 3 teaspoons Dijon mustard

2 tubes (10.20 ounces each) large refrigerated flaky biscuits

Instructions

1. In a large bowl, combine the cheese, ham, mayonnaise, bacon and mustard. Split biscuits into thirds. Press onto the bottom and up the sides of ungreased miniature muffin cups. Fill each with about 1 tablespoon of cheese mixture.

2. Bake at 450° until cups are golden brown and cheese is melted, 9-11 minutes. Let stand for 2 minutes before removing from the pans. Serve warm.

Nutrition Facts

2 ham cups: 134 calories, 8g fat (4g saturated fat), 20mg cholesterol, 436mg sodium, 9g carbohydrate (1g sugars, 0 fiber), 6g protein.

8. Reuben-Style Pizza

Ingredients

1 tube (13.8 ounces) refrigerated pizza crust

4 ounces cream cheese, softened

1 can (10-3/4 ounces) condensed cheddar cheese soup, undiluted

1/4 cup Thousand Island salad dressing

2 cups cubed pumpernickel bread

2 tablespoons butter, melted

1/2 pound sliced deli corned beef, coarsely chopped

2 cups sauerkraut, rinsed and well drained

1-1/2 cups shredded Swiss cheese

Instructions

1. Preheat oven to 425°. Unroll and press dough onto bottom of a greased 15x10x1-in. baking pan. Bake 6-8 minutes or until edges are lightly browned.

2. Meanwhile, in a small bowl, beat cream cheese, soup and salad dressing until blended. In another bowl, toss bread cubes with melted butter.

3. Spread cream cheese mixture over crust; top with corned beef, sauerkraut and cheese. Sprinkle with bread cubes. Bake 12-15 minutes or until crust is golden and cheese is melted.

Nutrition Facts

1 piece: 539 calories, 28g fat (14g saturated fat), 84mg cholesterol, 1939mg sodium, 48g carbohydrate (7g sugars, 4g fiber), 24g protein.

Made in the USA
Las Vegas, NV
25 February 2025

18627225R00038